This book is dedicated to our children, who inspired us to write and explore the wonderful world of food. This helped us to learn and enjoy our time together as a family.

We would also like to thank our parents Raymond and Comfort Leye, Jean-Piere and the late Lily Ifeko for always supporting us. Thank you to all those who have lent us a hand in some way, shape, or form on our journey of writing this book, Benedicte and Eric Mokonzo, Naomi, Michelle and Dara.

ISBN: 978-1-3999-6993-2

The moral right of the author has been asserted.

Book Design by Uzuri Designs
www.uzuridesignsbooks.com
bookdesigner@uzuridesignsbooks.com

Alphabet Foods

By Christelle
and Ezekiel Leye

Tips on how to read together

1. Schedule a time

2. Find a comfortable space

3. Make it fun

4. Take turns reading

5. Talk about what you read.

Tips on how to Eat together

1. Set time aside

2. Plan what you want to eat

3. Wash your hands

4. Help out with preparations
   or setting the table

5. Try each other's favourite foods

6. Discuss what you like about the food

7. Plan what you want to eat next time.

Apples

APPLES are shiny, **green** and **red**,
they feel smooth and are squeaky
says my Uncle Ted.
Sweet and juicy I love how they crunch.
Daddy's gone to the market
to bring some for lunch.

Bananas

Bananas are yellow just like the sun,
they feel quite rubbery, to eat them is fun.
Soft and sweet, to peel them is nice,
they are not only for monkeys,
what a delight!

B

C

Chowder is a type of soup or stew
often prepared with milk.
Its texture could be described
to be as smooth as the finest silk.

Dewberry

Dewberry is a blackberry-like fruit.
It can be eaten raw,
or even used to make pie.
If you'd like some then say I, I.

D

Eggs

Eggs have a shell
that is oh so delicate,
inside is a treat
that is not quite ready yet.

Fromage

Fromage in French
is the word for cheese.
Do you want some?
Then say 'oui oui'.

F

Grapes

Grapes come in three colours;
red, purple or green,
sweet and fresh
absolutely fit for a queen.

G

Hotdogs

Hot dogs are my favourite,
but please don't worry.
They are not really dogs
I was told by my mummy.

Ice-cream

Ice-cream is cold, sweet
and creamy,
if I have one too many
I can start feeling queasy.

Jelly

Jelly is delightful in my belly,
It tickles my tonsils,
it wiggles and wobbles.
That's what I call a treat,
I think it's really neat.

J

Kiwis

Kiwis feel rough and oh so hairy,
once you get through the skin
it's tangy and seedy.

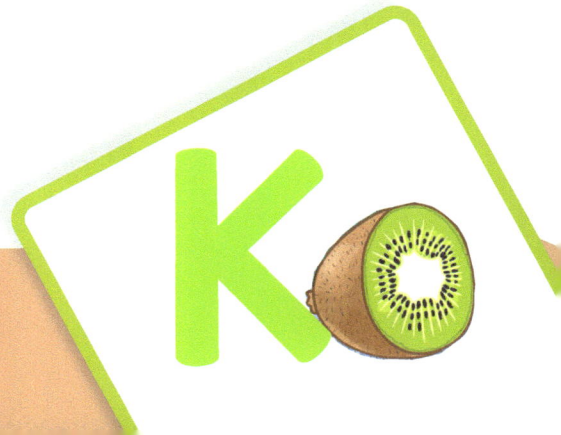

Lemons

Lemons are yellow and sour,
let's make lemonade
and have some in an hour.

Mangoes

Mangoes are smooth
Red, orange or green.
There's a party in your mouth
once you take off the skin.

Noodles

Noodles are long
and soft like string,
make them into a crown
so we can be Kings.

N

Oranges

Oranges are high in vitamin C,
they're great for football matches,
they can give energy.

Poblano Peppers

Poblano Peppers are not too spicy.

What a welcome relief

as I want them for curry.

P

Quiche

Quiche is delicious,
I will have mine with vegetables and fish.
Fluffy and light such a beautiful dish.

Q

Raspberries

R

Raspberries are fruity and healthy,
mix them together
for a tasty smoothie.

Salami

Salami is Italian,
just like my friend Gian.
He puts it on his pizza,
with extra mozzarella.

S

Tuna

Tuna I love in my pasta bake,
sometimes in sandwiches,
I just adore the taste.

Ugli

Ugli is a citrus fruit from Jamaica,
it's a cross between a tangerine
and a grapefruit.
It is just what I need
to get me in the dancing suit.

U

Vanilla

V

Vanilla, that's the secret to delightful cupcakes, some say they are plain but that's a mistake.

Wasabi

Wasabi is a green plant
that is usually served with sushi.
Spice up your life,
you can never be gloomy.

W

Xigua

Xigua is the Chinese word for watermelons.
Inside they are juicy and soft
but watch out for seeds.
The outside is firm
you can't break with a squeeze.

Yam

Yam is a great source of fibre
and also copper,
it's delicious and oh so nutritious.

Zucchini

Zucchini looks like a cucumber
and is shaped like a cylinder.
It grows in the summer, let's explore,
we could discover splendid flavours galore.

Z

www.ingramcontent.com/pod-product-compliance
Lightning Source LLC
Chambersburg PA
CBHW060814090426

42737CB00002B/58